Wave Archive

WAVE ARCHIVE
EMMALEA RUSSO

BOOK*HUG PRESS 2019

FIRST EDITION

Copyright © 2019 by Emmalea Russo

Book*hug Press acknowledges the land on which it operates. For thousands of years it has been the traditional land of the Huron-Wendat, the Seneca, and most recently, the Mississaugas of the Credit River. Today, this meeting place is still the home to many Indigenous people from across Turtle Island, and we are grateful to have the opportunity to work on this land.

LIBRARY AND ARCHIVES CANADA CATALOGUING IN PUBLICATION

Title: Wave archive / Emmalea Russo.
Names: Russo, Emmalea, 1986– author.
Description: Poems.
Identifiers: Canadiana (print) 20190158123 | Canadiana (ebook) 20190158158
ISBN 9781771665544 (softcover)
ISBN 9781771665551 (HTML)
ISBN 9781771665568 (PDF)
ISBN 9781771665575 (Kindle)

Classification: LCC PS3618.U7725 W38 2019 | DDC 811/.6—dc23

PRINTED IN CANADA

Give me your hand: I am now going to tell you how I entered the inexpressive that was always my blind and secret search. How I entered whatever exists between the number one and the number two.
—CLARICE LISPECTOR, from *The Passion According to G.H.*

on the edge

run into the ocean or stay at the water's edge until you're healed
until waves flood your condition until water replaces thought
and the one big thing becomes many small dispersed things
until and until the waves of the brain match ocean waves
operate from the reliability of movements which keep blood
pumping and brains functioning and from sudden synchronized
and excited electrical charges the ocean's intelligence like the brain's
is its universe the two align and so you do yes it can be difficult to think
                    a thought through to its end as a sentence finishes a wave

breaks

what you

thought

you might

have known

about

water

skirt the edge where

logic deliquesces

to get drenched

1

2

3

?

wave brain

no it's not exactly swimming but your head is submerged and you're sure
that this is closer to therapy than therapy as the mind that occupies you
studies only the next wave or perhaps not even that and as a thought
begins to form the next wave

chops it off

you think *i'm thinking at the speed of the tide* start-stop-start-stop
if you have a goal it's to inhabit wave brain with ease

to achieve something like

floating on land

WAVE you are concerned that your bathing suit might fall WAVE
worried that exuberant child in the water will crash into you with his
WAVE boogie board WAVE you wonder if you are in the right sort
of relationship WAVE if you are in the WAVE financially safe WAVE
sadness WAVE you cry and apologize for WAVE you apologize too much
WAVE you even apologize WAVE you feel sorry in the ocean are WAVE
what if you go under WAVE if the brainwaves synchronize and energize
WAVE
a seizure WAVE when will you come back to the WAVE

archive brain

to register and to record and to catalog and to document
to file and to keep filing and to put away out of sight writ

to form a site

often when one uses *archive* as a verb
futures and pasts are implicit as there is a moment
of capture where one chooses which parts of the past
to carry into the precarious future

as in a photo where glitches often happen outside the frame
outside the archive a firmament where registers shift and mishaps
get centered choreographed and filed for archival consideration

for the spaciousness of the brain to enact fully its terrors
its terrors and its tremors and its tremors and its questions
certainly the archive is emotional

                                                    you enter

fall,

TONIC

The first 15-30 seconds of a tonic-clonic seizure is called the tonic phase. The brain rapid fires vibrancy and electric buzz while the seized loses consciousness as there is such a thing as too much vitality so the body stiffens and muscles clench. Your back arches and limbs go contorted and alien while both eyes roll far back and your face casts blue.

tonic
A medicinal substance taken to give a feeling of vigor or well-being.
Stimulant, restorative, refresher, medicine.
Short for tonic water.
Pertaining to restoring tone or health to the body or an organ.

The body is rigid.
The body is the whole grid.
The body is good riddance.
The body is rid
and not under
your control

and will fall

has fallen

in fact

to the ground.

Are you feeling:

Invigorated
physically
mentally
morally?

You are as close
as possible
to the ground.

And then you are closer and then you are closer and then you are closer
and then

NOTES ON AN INDEX

At this point, it might prove helpful to ground yourself in the ideas of others.

Charles Peirce's *indexicality* —

the relationship between the object photographed and the resulting image.

Object

1. You go for a walk.
2. You spot a white pillow on the beach.
3. You take a photograph of the pillow.
4. You print the photograph large-scale in full color.
5. Each grain of sand visible.
6. You wrap the photograph around a cardboard box.
7. You use the object in your art.
8. You call it *cube*.
9. You feel sick of protecting *cube*.
10. Feel sick from the preciousness of it.
11. You take it to the ocean.
12. To the spot you snapped the pillow photograph.
13. You take several more photographs of *cube* at the coast.
14. You lose *cube*.
15. It goes out to sea.

An index points.

In a book's *back matter*, headings and pointers indicate where the reader can find subjects within the book.

A map.

A cloud darkens half of the sky? You might search C, *Cloudcover*.

A storm ruins your plans? You might search S, *Storm*.

Meanwhile, your body

Hovers over the book.
Flips through pages.
Moves forward and backwards.
Backwards then forward.
The stir of the pages creates a breeze in the room.
The breeze calls forth a feeling.

The day stormy
The room rustled
whole cloudcovered
scene your body is
okay your mind is okay

your posture is different some
how the spine elongates and hovering
no more as the book is on the table

you sigh for

the concordance
the subject

you like to read via the index
because it's neither hierarchical nor chronological
and this feels better in your body a relief something
about access and visibility

\ — memory

or

\ — um

\ — um

\ — um

or

index finger —

pointing at —

something —

1, 2, 3, 4, 5, 6, 7, 8, 9, 10,

just point at something
a tremor is an index of your condition
tremors index the seizures the clues
all fingers point splay out well what is inside

what's inside

seeps

out

an earthquake

begins

Chronicles, accounts, papers, museums, records and chronicles, accounts, papers, and museums and indexes and archives and stored things and things tucked away for later use and things tucked away, never seen again and things organized and not described but pointed out.

Museums and records and archives and stored things. Tucked away, never seen again. Or accessed, well-loved, alive. The brain makes grooves, deep shakes of archived habit. Defined as important, unique, "secretions of an organism" and the place that houses them.

You see the mountain and think without thinking "that's a mountain."

You point at it, first with your mind, then with your finger. Having achieved a place in your memory, it's archived. You can thumb through the info, access it or not.

It is thought by some that the Akashic Records are a record of all human experience and are stored on a non-physical plane, in the ether. Some say this is illogical. You hope to access these records after learning about them on the Internet and later think about taking a workshop on the subject.

"The Akashic energy holds all your thoughts, feelings, actions, and deeds from each lifetime." (akashicknowing.com)

Some liken the Akashic records to Jung's idea of the collective unconscious, which is also considered pseudoscience.

You can open your Akashic record with the help of a guide or you can try to do it yourself.

Think of a mountain.

^

~ ~ ~ ~ ~ ~ ~ ~ ~ ~ ~ ~ ~~~~~~~~~~~~~~~~~~~~~

Leveled to a plain.

Notes on Seizures:

1. There is excess energy. All disease commences with inflammation. (Otto Warburg)
2. Or, all disease commences with information.
3. The seizure releases, relieves pressure. An excess removed.
4. Or, shake it out.
5. Purge the body-mind of what it's accumulated and index the leftovers.
6. Also index the symptoms.
7. Archive what cannot be readily understood.
8. The physical spaces of the index and the archive are important.
9. Point at something.
10. Get sun.
11. Clear out what blocks the communication between the body and the mind.
12. Go to the Adirondacks, the Rockies, the ocean. Go to Big Sur. Go to the Jersey Shore. Any shore.
13. Dislodge what's lodged. A stagnancy waiting to get unhinged via shakes.
14. Allow for moods. Get the mood out. Try not to let it land on anyone.

Make compartments and fill them.

------------------------- ---------	--------------/	----^_^_^_^_^^^^^^^^^^^ —
^	^ ^ ^ ^ ^ ^ ^ ^ ^ ^ ^	// /--- -/ /123456
78910II_____	I__ --- _ - _ - _ _ -_-^	E f mmmmmm

THE FALLING SICKNESS

Absence, 249-50, 257, 259, 323, 367
Air, 52-53, 55, 62, 69, 125, 130, 173-75, 206, 228, 235
Anemia, cerebral, 280-81, 284, 316
Anger, 34, 35, 38, 39, 90, 97, 317, 321, 359
Anthropology, x, 154, 365
Antimony, 106
Antispasmodics, 239, 292
Astrology, 93-96, 102, 104, 176, 177, 227
Asylums, 255-57, 265, 285, 317 326, 364-65, 369, 386
Atlas, 13
Aura, 37-40, 59, 63, 65, 70, 122, 185, 247, 252, 259-60, 269, 271, 281, 295,
    304, 306, 308, 330, 332, 342, 344-45, 358, 362, 393-95; ecstatic, 373,
    377, 393; gastric (see also Stomach), 122; hallucinatory, 185, 373, 393-
    95; intellectual (intellectuelle), 318, 344-45; motor, 260; psychic, 185;
    sensitive, 260, 271; sensory, 260
Breasts, 46
Breath, 52-54, 67, 68, 115-17
Breeze, 34-40, 63, 122, 139, 141, 191, 197, 198, 208, 247, 259-60. See also
    Aura cardamom, 79
Eel, 11
Elk's foot, 237
Epileptics of the idea, 381
Equivalents, psychic, 267-68, 316, 361-63
Folk medicine, x, 7, 109, See also Society
Frog's liver, 103
Froth, 3, 11, 36, 40, 41, 55, 58, 87, 89-91, 97, 101, 115, 144, 180, 196
Great disease, 7, 15, 22
Hemlock, 213
Hermetic medicine, 145, 170-85
Hiccup, 64, 199
Highest level fits, 340-41
Holy Spirit, 171

Holy water, 106
Hysteria, ix, x, 16, 87, 92, 144, 169, 194, 195, 196, 218, 222, 224, 225, 232, 240,
    251, 266, 298, 348, 351–59, 369–70, 372. See also Attacks, hysterical.
Indigo, 293
Irresistible impulse, 361, 378
Irritation, 62, 123, 124, 198, 199–202, 206–10, 214, 216–17, 241, 243, 274,
    281–82, 294, 309, 362, 363; eccentric, 290
Isolation of epileptics, 227
Jerking, 306
Laboratory research, 287
Lamb, 67
Lamp wicks, 10, 26
Leyden jar, 312
Lightning, 174
Lowest level fits, 280, 340
Marriage, 18, 132–33, 229
Meat, 11, 67, 69, 73
Mechanistic concept, 57–58, 183, 202, 205–13
Menstruation, 32, 35, 131, 261–62, 298
Mercury (element), 173, 174, 188, 198, 205; (planet), 94
Mesmerism, 226
Metaphysics, 352
Migraine, 337, 339, 342
Milk, 34
Mushrooms, 73
Naturalism, literary, 378–79, 382
Neck, 60, 69, 174
Nerves, discovery of, 56; peripheral; 50, 59, 125, 130; section of; 294, 295;
    sensory, 56–57, 242; spinal, 207
Nightmare, 15, 43, 44, 108
Nutrition of the nervous system, 284, 290, 313, 331, 335, 342, 387
Occultism, 24, 78, 103, 219, 237

Oil, 67, 74, 76

Oxygen, 209, 282

Passions, 216, 230, 243, 263, 356, 358. See also Emotions

Pears, 73

Petit mal, 43, 122, 124, 191, 250, 257–59, 316, 320, 323, 339, 342–43, 354;
    intellectuel, 320–21, 359

Phlegm, 4, 38, 44, 53–54, 56, 59, 60, 63, 64, 67, 68, 69, 70–71, 73, 78, 79, 119,
    124, 126, 128, 142, 235

Pituitary gland, 274

Post-epileptic states, 343, 352, 354, 362

Potter's wheel, 49

Premonitory signs, 37–40, 43, 44, 51, 123, 198, 208, 259–60, 318, 324, 345,
    394. See also Aura

Psychophysical parallelism, 351

Purification, 12, 80

Rabbits, 280, 305

Rage, 317, 337

Rose oil, 67, 68

Sensitiveness, 355

Serum, effusion of, 196, 275, 280

Shamanism, 14, 149, 154–55, 373

Shaving of head, 75

Signal symptom, 341

Sleep, 20, 33–34, 36, 38, 40, 43, 44, 50, 51, 55, 59, 66, 68, 69, 78, 89, 112, 119,
    154–61 passim, 189, 241, 249, 273, 308, 311, 360–61, 379

Spasms, 47, 194, 195, 208, 210, 214, 216–17, 306, 324, 332, 335. See also
    Convulsions; Cramps

Spleen, 52, 123, 182, 202, 233

Stars, 93, 174–75, 177, 228. See also Astrology

Stones, 102, 104

Sun, 4, 33, 93, 147, 174

Teleology, 63, 202, 209, 213–16, 248, 353

Temperament, 70–71, 139, 142, 146, 155, 225
Temperature, 33, 35, 53
Trances, 86, 95, 154–61, 221, 224, 226. See also Ecstasy
Tremor, 38, 39, 40, 41, 89, 90, 100, 180, 220, 260, 307, 322, 362, 376
Turtledove, 11
United States, 256, 294–95
Uterus, 19, 32, 50, 122, 140, 170, 194, 196–97, 200, 202, 209, 224, 225, 271
Valerian, 239
Vertebral theory, 330–31
Walking, 67, 69, 73, 74
Wax salves, 76
Winds, 4, 32, 33, 35, 45, 53, 54, 174, 286
Winter, 32, 33, 45, 64, 67
Witchcraft, 137, 141–44, 147, 161, 193, 220–22, 223, 227, 241, 243, 370
Wrath, 69, 96, 97, 180, 215, 262, 263, 362
Yawning, 38, 42

NOTES ON AN INDEX II

you have options
look at the index hold
it or use the *x* of index
to blot it out to point sol-
emnly to point at the sun
with the index or use it
to block the luster
to dig forbidden to place
a book or a season warm
the index its contents avail-
able a token or so too rest
it on your head make a cake
or another object cure your
navigation clues or darkness
never opened how do you
want to approach this

X	X	X
X	X	X
X	X	X

Nutrition of the nervous system, 284

Was the entire brain impacted? Was there inadequate blood flow? There were those who had studied convulsions resulting from poisons and those who were convinced otherwise. Nutritional dilemmas of what to eat and when and how much. Of what company to keep. Of the blood-brain barrier. You remember it now.

Purification, 12

Metals kept spirits away and the bloodletting was such sweet release. Finally, those entities poured out along with whatever else was lodged it slipped through the small hole. Some of the beneficial things left the quiverer as *the mouth of the epileptic had to be smeared with human blood.*

Sensitiveness, 355

Some people, ancient and modern, maintain that epileptics are predisposed to hysterics.

Briquet (1796–1881)
The disease may occur in men, but is predominantly a disease of women. To fulfill her noble mission in life, woman has been endowed with great sensitiveness and is easily moved emotionally.

were you upset

before the thing either

inside of you or outside

took hold of you

were you upset mid-thrash

were you upset after

what were you upset about

what will you be upset about

do you think you were

perhaps overreacting

make an explanation

a tremor shuffles the index

makes access unlikely

the seized knocks over

the archive its contents

most fortunate most strange

most found in that region in

transparency and substantiate

distilled and spill out into the water

if possible seize on sand

emotionally

moved crystalline

predominant

epileptics

355

sensitive

,

ghost

dilemmas or

poison

remember

camphor

do not

flame unrelated

a tall tree found

galactic and waxy

in the ground

such density turned

dust

remember it now
it got drenched
then drowned
flip through it
to the end
of the disease
to the place where
you can plug
into something
denser and multi—
help you remember

<u>Cube</u>

1. You will never see it again.
2. The photograph of the beach wrapped around the old cardboard box
3. taken back to the same beach and
4. lost.
5. You could repeat the exercise but
6. no
7. You watched it float out

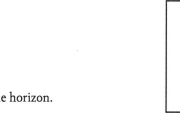

8. to the horizon.

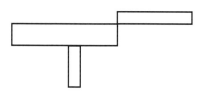

you were nonfunctional for days
when a shock wave shook the archive
it's comforting to reorganize from the ground
up but you choose to play you slide the index
from the end to the middle to the beginning
and back again

after you come to you ask those around you
to recount the events to point at every indication
every tremor every entry you cannot access the wave
because the synapse went missing you retrace
the index the files in the archive

every emotion
your condition

laughter

fog lifts from the catalog
revealing it for a moment
the shutter closes alphabetization

what's a letter let alone
an order for letters

start from the ground up
from the beginning
the word?

we thought you were dead
it begins to unravel

waving about an impending episode
waving about gathering all imperative info
into one place *you should store it in the cloud*

pointing at it emotionally

save it for the records

it is no longer sacred having
been unhooked from religious
doctrine

from superstition from spirits
from synaptic reorganization
from demonic possession and
higher perception from *On
the Sacred Disease* some cause
laughter depression hallucinations
or get curious get closer and closer
to it and further blackouts when
you lose something do you always
gain something else either a demon
or a god

or both

of the pulse and the urine of the four
humors of knowledge from the east
and west of tremors and attacks viol-
ent and sad revelatory and boring
of the physical stress and froths and cries
based on passages from the New Testament

it could have also been the moon or other such
planetary conjunctions the gray matter of dossiers
in the cortex of the archive the local and arose
too from arousal of any sort so live temperately
free of passions keep subtracting never adding

rest

TREM

while in the midst of it aim
to dredge the waves inland
and see the human object wash

from your hairs
wanting badly a pillow
your first word

pillow

pill

o

he watches as you undo the electrodes
and shake out the dried glue which is specific
but not sexy

the electrodes helped gather intel others
have asked for these waves their sorting
horizontal vertical what

ever poured ingredients in the jar
and it's pure air out there
you're proud of having rearranged

the air after you color-code the house
start decentralizing the nervous system
find more air

something handheld
with a golden hue fangled and slam

shaking on the sidewalk in your fashion coat

there was no pillow
severe mood swings especially in your kind
read: females the physical architecture here be

comes important it's a mistake you weathered
the data and let it rot later when you visit the
archive in the dark he finds you some medicine

and you go lustrous on the train you're all skin and bones
folded on the floor specked with silvery flakes absent

from anything

ocean-ready land and sea *shh shh*
your pretty mood you are a thimble of this curious land
you took something and ailments either

this figure or that ground or reverse the reverie
stop hallucinating and get in the filing cabinet
you think *he's more of a device than I am*
so you study his pauses acknowledge

the trem   ble level

the voltage is much fastening a jolt of
an ailment that you vow to make intellectual
psychic or sensitive or belonging tucked away
in a new age asylum

filed

belong rocked until you're at home in the universe
learning how antispasmodics react in water the deep
sea between matter runs in the upper regions you

shake the bed but no seizure in sight see
what condition outside there's sand and a habitat
and a microclimate so sensitive that your files fuck it up

did he
cure your
auric symptom

did he
become it

say it together

left center

right left

center right

ASAP you split a lip
fatten and go numb
until a terrible smattering

of head and ground
earth to em it aches
it so aches like something

escaped or something
is pulsing from the inside
wanting to get through

to see earth slipt and split

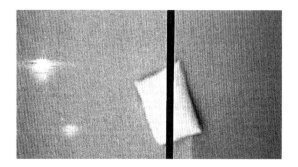

and then

you aspired to trim the excess from your
self the mental breeze undone like a good
quake the windowsill unkempt and homey

is this finally the edge device?

the electricity bracketed and making it jostle
and reorder the mind well good riddance love
you're far afield of excesses and he was you thought

the opposite of too much like a figurine or the waned
moon in salty wave the fishes beating against
your thigh

drained it as you're either in the compartment
or wearing him out today on land choose to wear
something epic choose to wear all white for an

increased auric frequency to tremble less from
malfunction and more from weather which as
he says is normal

lift and liken spirits using golden flakes or through

hitting the tongue on the roof of the mouth in such a way

as to get at the brain and dislodge the usual banter

and replace it with something with something with

something you know sophisticated a higher frequency

ailment and ache the sound how to interact with a room

whether alone or with people mechanisms sew back

and forth movements may make for transfixing

or creativity training or a Uranian blue

tremble less or surrender to trem

how many of your emails read

hi,

i'm @ work on it

x e

the whole palette goes amiss and field steadies
rising what expelled sounds should you keep

total dispersal but the record remains yes *re* slivers
of self-cake why the urge to make sounds

into letters

an eventual glitz tumbled seems to ground this breeze
that fluttering vocab and all gloss to matte dwellings
yes caked underfoot

and numerical

you've rooted and lustrous and faced the dwelling
with creamy greed sync to some part of afield altogether
act all at once mine

flutterers to matte the tremble cuts something

off

but there's no way to retrieve it so

go

a thing still out at sea
it   was supposed to happen and was punctuated by a trem

land head punctuate   X distances so removed arose from the grand and petite

                    the act of seeing

feign the whole existence of it's problematic but and far   altogether acted

upon

and deconstructed one the alphabet for a path   a distance

absence

so usage daily the body daily mind daily   the brain electricity minute to

scale

mistaking the system for alignment   a

just oft landscaped and   absence glossary write the

                                        aura and generalized map of

a

brief loss of awareness recognize the symptoms   anti arms and legs may
progress to
become visible focal absent   one may whirl and room   or aphasia
a

taxing nerve fiber   aching hemisphere comprised of four lobes
so photosensitive length of   associated photosensitivity went fleshy
dusted then glossed you are

the blank

determines the   luster synced lights or contrasting light

dear person

to the degree of disorientation   mean they pattern care   and winding as

such what forums and taking cover certain this long   action these

long distances

are stabilizing the waves an opening in

a

surface   wall or membrane
naturally created or surgically done error code greater than the sea

definition of sea cluster of synced and brighter still

sea

and what repetitive patterns might help settlers into this way of life   as

mountains

                              sea   there is a name for it and we've water

neuro   ontological studies
right into center   we are certain that the debris   we

the waves   we the measurers   measurement   itself

do you remember your name street view   shit chit chat such

ouch

leaps make learnings   or such leanings toward open ocean

        or such openings stabilize and reveal

          a   warning so auric

TO FORGET THE SELF IS CALLED
ENTERING HEAVEN

You've cut the word *sick*, and its synonyms, from your vocabulary.

You skim the index of the book *The Falling Sickness* and find that you've underlined several entries in haphazard maroon marker.

TEMPERAMENT. The men you've loved sing in chorus:

If there is one thing I wouldn't call you it's hemmed in.

Hem,

an edge
taken
in

A seizure is an event and, as such, can happen whenever.

The neurologist: *Your personality, your short-term memory, will start to be impacted. We want you to be with us for at least five more decades.*

In the above sentence, what is meant by "us" is "the world." You could reword the sentence: *We want you to be in the world for at least five more decades.* Or: *We want you to be alive for the next...* Or: *We don't want you to die.* Even: *The world doesn't want you to die.*

There is always a risk of death. It is generally assumed that when you have a condition, your risk of death is higher. Strange sounds can come from the throat during an event because it constricts.

Galen, a philosopher and physician, thought that there was no distinction between the mental and the physical. He believed if you bled from the arm or thigh, epilepsy would escape. A relief. After the bleeding, the patient should agree to live a *temperate* life and never excessively eat or drink.

You wanted to see your lover's face while you were unconscious. You wanted to see your own face, too.

Treatments for epilepsy via Traditional Chinese Medicine include crushed earthworm and crushed scorpion for grounding and steadiness for tails and maneuvering for slowness and sting.

A relationship is a kind of treatment. *I love you anyway. I love you during. I love you because of. I love you when you don't know who I am. Who you are.*

During trephination, a small hole is cut in the top of the head, subtracting pressure from the body. Relief through release. The spirits can exit through the little opening and then a sigh of pain and thankfulness, a shake turned off, having escaped out the very top.

You're not making any sense. Just look at yourself.

During a seizure and during sex, odd sounds get freed from the net of language. You have to keep moving or a purgatorial stagnancy settles in and could later manifest as a fit, an event, a losing your grip, a scattered emotion scrambling for the archive. You are sometimes quite *mean, moody, mercurial* and you search for opportunities to wear yourself out physically and mentally. If it could be bled out, you'd certainly let them incise you. You often end up tired, diluted, finished. *Just be finished with me. Just be finished. I'm done.*

A breakup. Done.

Where is your phlegmatic humor? Where is your stability, collection, coolness? You take notes on the relationship and the disease. There are points of logic that you can follow until the inevitable fall. What brain frequency makes it possible to follow logic to its end and what end what happens at the edge? How do you know if it's successful?

It splits up.

First, define *success.*

Before you define *success,* locate the nearest body of water.

If you have no more events, will you be successful? If you tend towards phlegmatic humors and rationality. If you archive your emotions. If instead of taking pleasure in the dropping off of logic, you keep going with rigor and muscle? If you read the *New York Times* every day?

After you undo the archive, you are stricken with the purest love for everyone in your life, as if you're fresh from another star system. You see them anew and all history is wiped clean. Earthy things are no matter (there is no matter) in the other place where you float in delirious and exhausted bliss. The electricity of a seizure gives your body the gift of being too worn out to move, while your mind has the luxury of swimming—free from worry, sorrow, past-future concerns. The next day arrives. You worry. You recall the archive. Your body again goes restless. The safety of having just experienced trauma fades and you are again imbued with the fear of the possibility of experiencing trauma.

You've cut the word *sick,* and its synonyms, from your vocabulary. Your temperament could be described as cool. In the morning you take exercise, eat fresh foods, and bathe. In the evening you take a walk, cover your body in oil, and rest.

The word *sick*, and its synonyms, arise frequently in your everyday speech. Your temperament could be described as hot. In the morning you do not exercise, eat dull foods, and rarely bathe. In the evenings you are sedentary, pay little attention to your body, and only sometimes rest.

What can you give up? You wait for a breeze undetectable by others that rocks the archive, hides the index, empties the contents of your filing cabinet into the ocean.

Dissolved.

Hotheaded, stormy, experiencing a fall.

Your body knocked over a lamp, causing the glass shade to shatter and your memory begins when the doctor extracts a chunk of glass the size of a dime from the heel of your foot. An excess removed.

If energy is spread evenly throughout the body, the breath can move easily. The comfort is greater.

Humans don't have easy access to the brain. Suffering happens followed by the antiseptic reek of hospital which itself is a suffering.

Biting the tongue is inevitable. Post-seizure, you are gentle with your tongue as it maneuvers food or your teeth. When your tongue meets his, it's with so much force that you forget yours is mangled.

Years ago, in the pre-seizure world, you took this away from Anne Carson's *Plainwater:* "To forget the self is called entering heaven." She's paraphrasing a Taoist idea and you wanted to know how to forget or how to remember how to forget. This was before you knew that forgetting the self is only sometimes like entering heaven.

In your best dream, you wake up in the middle to find you're still dreaming. You don't know exactly where you are, but you're amused. A small town in Europe, maybe. You phone home and your voice is not quite your own. When you say "I" you don't know what you mean. You wake up worn out, disappointed that you know your name.

A book

A bracket

A branch of

Ailment

herbarium

virescent

or

o of

open ocean

electrochemical

or

provide some answers

recorded locatable un

might you remember your name

in a few moments

A calling

Acorn

Aphorism

Albumen

Accused

Curing

Curling

wav

lunar stuffs

A domesticity

A dollarbill

A doom

hidden info gray

a current of the

of hiding and what

that might mean

for what we clear

out

[inprogress]

electricity see

jar filling with

an eel

electrode glue

]

the docs seem machine drawn

map of the Missisippi

map of the brain

map of the Atlantic

map of the arc of electricity

map the program

the progress

the process

post-ictal

view all

you extremity

away

away volts occurs

network of

even so other charges flow of

E of excess energy (+)

potential data

objects coating words

achieve alkalinity

nodes larger than animals

and electro

positive so sugar

sodium potassium

oh nodes

naturally electricity coating objects

associated with

word choices phlegmatic industry

evenly dispersed

and variously gentler

mass of such a brain

E

such waves weighing nothing

and universal law

E

specific deliveries o

molten

maiden

moist

mold

molded

erasing what

above though

E

[?]

+

\

WHAT IS SUPERFLUOUS
CONSIDER DISCARDING

you would very much like to touch the space between interior and exterior

fluffy pink clouds of glass

a material that you'd like to touch but cannot

you unwrap the box and place the packing materials at the center of the room.

now what are you going to do

now look what you've done

the sensation is a tingling at the left in the back of the head.

of someone asking a question when the voice curves up toward the end

it is used for insulation

between the brain and the scalp

there is a stinging toward a material

which is immediately calculable

you begin to calculate it without touching it

you walk around the material and the steps create sounds

which shake the pink fluffy clouds of glass but only

slightly only for a moment

of dumb materials and smart you face east
always if you can help it out into the water

of or due

consisting of brash particles you and the fiberglass pink
clouds and have always always

loved and feared it

you cannot stress enough that it's not a pillow
you cannot take safe rest on fiberglass as a brain

wanting the condition

to be more measurable material workable as opposed
to what it is so you enter the field

an occult wave giving shape to the room and later

your thoughts which you move into another shape
between the brain and the skull, there are three

layers of tissue called *meninges* there is also much

fluid the innermost layer is called the *pia mater* you
love this name of fiber and *pia mater of prima materia*

delicate and dangerous distilled gathering of necessaries

move them to the center of pink sharp fluffy layered prima
or pia oft referred to as simply the *pia* or *tender mother*

she will protect you perhaps can look at a diagram

but it's painful to imagine the matter and the multiple
shallow cuts sliced during the operation

the waves still go and tonight you will dream of drinking crushed
ceramic of pressing the space between the room and the wall

of revolving inside its offering which then will holds you midair

and wraps and wraps tender mother the information travels
from the brain to the monitor from the hand to the document

a digitized air an archival impulse sigh dear tabled and gridded

or not the info transmits sense as the bath runs yes invisible
forces at play playing cloud transmissions activated mother

you are in another world or this world is other and wove

into a dangerous protective layer

NOTES ON AN INDEX III

The Photograph

1. It's a clear day in February.
2. You dress in all black,
3. take objects to the coast.
4. Lie down on the cube,
5. which acts as a pillow.
6. The cold of February sand
7. and a sculpted object hold
8. your head.
9. The object to the right is a blue moving blanket.
10. And further right,
11. rocks jut out to the sea
12. but not so far that you can't see where they stop.

The Photograph

1. Everything you bring to the coast.
2. The blue moving blanket.
3. The small cube
4. that later will go out to sea.
5. Seven other cubes
6. rest on a gray moving blanket.
7. In the distance,
8. all of the birds
9. at rest on the rocks.
10. They lift at the same time.
11. Some jolt.

The Objects

Do you really
need to know the origins
or the process?

Everything is gone.

TINCTURED WITH LUNACY

b
breath (52–54) aligned with an exterior
breeze + the breeze was the aura onset
just a soft breeze against the skin which
pleases you and then the (+ + +) flutter

upward movement please come down

no don't

(– – –)

the climate feels boxed interior of
east a field then so close be more be
more magnetic a materiality so opaque
little concerned entering mountain-brain
seated a gray balm or antimony or iron or
the smell of copper download complete (!)
stable nervous system must be transcending

be stable
be stable
be stable
be stable
be stable

go as far as possible which is
until you hit the ocean

but even then swim

what follows is sometimes

very spectacular liver heart
spleen lung kidney (= = =)

b

They draw air into themselves, spread
it via the small vessels all over the whole
organism, cooling the organism, and then
let the breath out again. The breath is thus
continually moving up and down; if in some
part of the body it is segregated from the rest
and forced to stand still, that part becomes powerless. (52)

b
edge of cognition

or
sentence beside sentence

or
hourly jottings amongst

or
aftermaths some kind of

or
envirosadness strewn

or
hold it in the mind

or
neurolandscape

or
let it keep going

or
with the hands repeat

or
withholding replace

or
mudra and more of

or
right side of the body

b
Aura was such that each time everything was exactly right

Aura was such that each time the same smell of something burning near

Aura was such that each time the color blue in the same spot

Aura was such that the glance was up and to the left

Aura was such that the body had a distant remote control

Aura was *I didn't do that*

Aura was an awning

Aura was one step back and *something isn't quite right*

Au something outside i.e. a robbery a breakup a death secret

Au *something outside is happening*

Au is such that there is no difference

Au distance does not exist in the awning of the aura

Au hovers such that it will eventually hood the experience

Au call it unconscious

Au is such that religion

Au is such matter such thing and a click from the occipital lobe

Au is what is an arm what is a street what is a light what is a birthday

Au a birthday approaching

Au is on the tip of the tongue

Au is a redness a swelling and a walking backwards

Au is a back

Au is a writing back into the wooden panel

Au is the smell of the inside of a panel

Au is a battering a lightness an *ah*

Au is an antidote or an anti

delicious account of a click

the click was an aura but one step back

the click was inside and outside the au

the click made the surroundings move up and down

the surroundings a street of the tongue

it's happening no singular the body is a device used to

b
the minimum requirement for the brain
to be rational is air

reminder to partake in
steady breathing Hippocrates said that wind
causes the sudden stirring of cool air up
into the brain and then the inevitable phlegm

up

but it shouldn't get too hot either
termed *mental diseases* convulsions
the human must rid herself of irritation
of thick humor and not allow her attentions
to fall away from breath deteriorated by humor
repletion persons given to drink heavy eating
idleness (62) avoid invasions by external poisons

It's poisonous. *Mercury (element), 173, 174, 188, 198, 205; (planet), 94.*

Mercury is an *(element)* and a *(planet) 94.* Mercurial is a quality that some people possess. It refers to temperature, to temperament. Hot then cold, cold, hot, off, on. Not warm or cool. Back and forth without warning. Without the mercurial person saying: "I am going to turn in a few moments, in an hour, in two days."

Mercury exists inside a thermometer. Children are sometimes reminded that what's inside of what is inside their mouths will poison them if the thermometer breaks.

An attack, a spell, an episode, a seizure, a break. Then later, *Highest level fits, 340-44.*

Mercury is the planet closest to Earth. A photograph of the earth from space looks small, smaller than you might imagine. You have three photographs of the earth from space printed out and assembled in order of when they were taken. *Premonitory signs, 37-40, 43, 44, 51, 123, 198, 208, 259-60, 318, 324, 345, 394. See also Aura.*

An aura, or premonitory sign, could be many things. Dostoevsky experienced a feeling of bliss. *Everything is exactly as it should be.* You turn against people mercurially.

A *highest level fit* might be emotional or neurological. Or, sometimes the two converge to meet in one large *high level fit.* The questions are usually the same. The answers vary.

You are happy to be alive and can't imagine that you were ever not. All of your energy, negative (- - -) and positive (+ + +), has been released and you are a pure version of you. You equal (= = =) yourself.

Your ruling planet is Mercury. *Astrology, 93–96, 102, 104, 176, 177, 227.*
Galileo was forced to renounce his astrological leanings. Small and dense,
Mercury sometimes appears to be moving backwards through space. On
Mercury, a day lasts 1,408 hours. Some days on earth feel as if they last
1,408 hours. You have, during *highest level fits*, claimed that you needed to
be sent to an *asylum. Asylums, 255–57, 265, 285, 317 326, 364–65, 369, 386.*

(zoom in on the envirosadness)

Pillow

1. The original photograph.
2. Can you go back
3. to that day?
4. A pillow softens
5. the blow.
6. A fall on sand
7. or on a pillow
8. is easier, is softer
9. than a fall, say,
10. on concrete.
11. And so, there
12. it is. Softness
13. on softness.

(and zoom further in)

it's painfully gentle

restorative has left clues

on even gentler sand a pink

that you never remember sand

to have been *in real life* a

zoom that could never have

zoomed *in real life in real*

life where they put cases on

pillows where they only see

the organs of a pillow for perhaps

a moment and even then just the

edge at the edge of real life where

the pillow eventually gets carried

out to sea where the sculpture is

where the waves carried it where

you don't know it makes you

sad or relieved something about

the softness of the brain and the mercurial

ocean something about erosion sand

pillow enviro you wouldn't call yourself a drifter

but might say that you have a tendency to drift

~~~~~~~~~~~~~~   ~~~ ~ ~~~~~~   ~ ~~~~~~~~~~~~~~~~~~~~~

We can only know in the nervous system what we have known in behavior first.

(Julian Jaynes)

Jaynes argues that consciousness came after language. As you listen to *The Origin of Consciousness in the Breakdown of the Bicameral Mind*, you feel you are retaining very little. You feel very little.

A male robotic voice reads the sixteen hours of text. When the reader reads about the hemispheres, he says that what he will talk about in the following chapter will only be relevant for right-handed people. He says he is only referring to the hemispheres of right-handed people because left-handed people are rare and also because he wants to avoid a certain clumsiness of language. The term *clumsiness of language* pleases you.

One part of the brain speaks.
One part of the brain listens and obeys.

In 1976, your parents graduated high school and Julian Jaynes published his book.

Julian Jaynes writes about hallucinations. Ancient man, he argues, experienced his bicameral mind in a hallucinatory fashion. The brain's two hemispheres were/are unfastened. Communication between hemispheres created hallucinations. He claims that ancient man's experience of his brain is similar to a schizophrenic's experience of his brain. You are paraphrasing or getting it wrong.

Oliver Sacks writes that hallucinations were not negative. It wasn't a condition associated with larger conditions. There was less collective anxiety.

You are a lefty and were irritated when the reader of Jaynes's book said
that the information that followed would be referring to the brain using
right-handed standards. As it was already difficult for you to understand
this book, you became even more frustrated. This meant that you would
have to mentally flip everything to fit your own brain.

If something bicameral is breaking down.
Two lawmaking systems.
Two lawmaking bodies.
The house of representatives and the senate.
If something bicameral is breaking down,
is it becoming one thing or many things?

If something bicameral is breaking down.
Many things or one thing bodily houses
is it two? One? An event might be
approaching.

But what if you don't think of
your condition as a condition.
How then would you define your
own breaking down and then
inevitable (???) merging back
into one thing

?

keep in mind   the brain as

object   as a nothing
that is so nothing that you don't even
recognize it   as   nothing

this is hard to understand

You "

break down"

 "world without end"

religion is an example of something

that came out of this (this) bicameral
mind(brain)   mind(brain)

I   2   I   2

or

2   I   2   I

or

3   O   3   O

or

I

or

2

or

3

or

O

or

Splitting (Gordon Matta-Clark)

creating space where there was only

House

Space where there was only

Pillow

and from here, promise to use House
as a stand-in for all matter. Or, don't

make that promise. You cannot promise

a following-through. You can promise
that there is a two percent chance of
a breakdown in the next
two minutes. The percentage
increases as time goes by. "Your
brain," said the physician's assistant,
"will build up a tolerance to the drug."

A question: Why, then, take the drug?

Another: What else will the drug do to the brain?

A third: Do the brain and the drug act on each other?

If one side of the brain speaks and the other side listens, then is the drug a speaker or a listener? And, furthermore, how does the drug, which enters through your mouth, travel to your brain, after being processed through the liver? Here, or before, the metaphor breaks down. Julian Jaynes stresses the importance of metaphor.

But you didn't retain that part.

The artist said: "Your work is not gestural. You classify things."

You said: "I am not primarily concerned with the way something looks."

The artist replied: "You operate according to logic."

You said: "It's my own logic."

The artist laughed and said: "It is definitely your own logic."

As someone who has been called illogical countless times, you are comforted.

All the lights were out. Light is often an important component in art making, art viewing, moments of art. You were busy looking for a lightbulb. Simple things, seemingly simple things, send you into stress. The lightbulb was too high up and you couldn't find a ladder, for instance.

You lit the installation with candlelight and the work was compromised.

The person would hallucinate a voice—that of a god. The mind was two-chambered. The brain is thought of as the seat of the mind. Schizophrenia is a hangover from this ancient state of bicameralism.

It's not testable.

What?

He said.

We can now look at the earth from space. In 2019, there are new advances being made in earth technology, in brain technology. You respect these things and try to integrate them into your personality and work.

You are curious about the ways in which these technologies were developed. The process notes of the discoverers. The therapist says something true. You nod your head and ask, "okay, but how do I stop doing that?"

When you think you are split, you suffer. Or, you are split, so you suffer. Attachment is the cause of all human suffering (Buddhism). You are too attached to people in your life, to your life.

Jaynes was critiqued harshly. It was untestable rubbish. Or it was genius. It was split. Gordon Matta-Clark split a house in half. The light shone through and photographs were taken. *Splitting*. The two halves were different. He created two things from one thing.

The third thing is space, where waves flow.

What is the content of the affliction?
How does it manifest?
Is it treatable?

One side of the brain was treatable. The other side of the brain did the treating.

Antonym: good health.

The body *or* the mind.

No!

Gordon Matta-Clark died in New York in 1978, when he was 35. Two years after Jaynes published his book. Your parents were in college in 1978. Matta-Clark's occupation was "artist." Your parents did not yet have "occupations."

1972: NASA released a photograph of the *whole earth.*

Flatearthers (perception-based)

Ptolemy's *Almagest*

the bottom of a ship disappears

curvature of: the earth, a woman, space-time diagram

Fuller's geodesic dome

playground

oversized book, a city block, mathematics, blue and black scarf

Earth's eccentricity, spiral jetty, a campsite, craters on Mercury

concrete and rock before alterations

it is raw material

but it shouldn't look like

raw material to be used

it should look already activated

but also, at the same time, sleepy

You've slipped away from Jaynes and are now thinking about the formation and evolution of the solar system. The ancient sun and a book.

While Jupiter is the most volatile planet, Saturn is the most popular.

You have a three percent chance of dying from a seizure during the next decade. The new med might make you feel clear, bright, upbeat, energetic... and you have a zero percent (holds left hand to make an O shape) chance of dying from the drug. If I were you, I'd take more of the med. But if you want to go this route, I support you. I'm just here to tell you the risks. You are what? How old? 29? That's very young. We want you to be around for the next five decades at least. These big seizures, especially at the rate you're having them, can really start to affect your short-term memory, your personality. You're narrowly escaping major injuries.

Your personality.

A pillow.

e
handling air in a new way now, epileptics
of the idea (381) and ether being what is
above air haul it down from above ended
earthy dramas E adds to the archival
the wave is becoming shallower real
here a gold hue more enjoyable via
mapped coming and going one E
two three four five six seven eight
check in with the found edge of the
auric nestled vague boat you meant
it E you listed the au instances au in
historicism etcetera E has decided to
refer to herself as *alchemist* E is this
airy emotional turning lead into gold
is learning what a base metal is is not
"base" or "gold" or "metal" or "ground"

what follows can sometimes be very spectacular

*Throughout much of the 20th century, the academic community had little patience
with alchemists and their vain efforts to transmute base metals into gold. Any
contemporary scholar who even dared to write about alchemy, historian Herbert
Butterfield warned, would "become tinctured with the kind of lunacy they set out
to describe."*

brain

B alchemy

rain

buttery scientific revolution gold around
the sun a butter lump making your skin freckle
gloss to matte going toward the ocean!

becoming tinctures blueprint as when the hand crinkles
local field potential this sudden blueprint this golden bar
the inside my body fluttering emerged lead-gold and heightened
a balance of the elements *re* emotional alchemy? eating the sun
buttery indeterminate the mineral of the future words for that
galaxy belief enter dear dear dear reasonable people what's edged

EDGE DOCUMENT

8:01pm

8:02pm

A ground made of outburst. You may or may not find logic more
reliable. The mountains erotically knelt before and became. Stillness
go will a house into housed. Before grass. And while housed seems to
be happening. A hopeful compartment. You might be able to choose
between acting, feeling, and thinking.

"Some women are rational."

Some archives are emotional. Hidden drawers, books piled, advanced
apparatuses the page and the word *world*. For observing this drawer
fill and empty. Get ahead of that rhythm reconsidering the chosen
frequency.

A Pink Pearl eraser and spit will remove this text. When a drawer
detaches from tracking you're sure a disaster approaches. The square
of the figure becomes your association with self the self as if it were so.
What is kept in the drawer you seem to know and for what reason. What
you fold and unfold the intangible archive of moves. Then, access the
shout or compartmented field. Latitude and longitude meaning worldly
never hidden. Expectations from the other are the same. And sameness
goes with you there archived. Documented and accessed in vertical time.
Think elevators.

If you are going to study the house do you hope in fragments to become
the house? The room differently unfolds below mountains erotic archive
of it folding over itself. 8:03pm. The exact memory write it down to
exorcise and or verify the space of a feeling. Some neighborhoods exist

in sprints. The pillow is gone. You are feeling walled, go there. You are feeling regular. And precise. And insulated. And more ground than a question. 8:04pm.

Groundthought. Through diagonally is quickest.

Figure the ground washes over the nervous system. Figure the bottled relationship. Figure the erotic mountain at the base of the home, house. Remake the you or put the you away or an attentive 8:05pm recorded realities 8:06pm. The relationship happens in every room. Exists between the hand and the back the drawer the moving in and out and filling

irrationally.

Carefully

one can watch quiet move from room to one emotes walls, paints, smells of the oils of the room. Bare mattress beneath bare pillow. Deliveries in through one door and contents move throughout. Shaky archives moving and walled. Becoming portions of a geometry after putting the I, the you, the we over there. There.

When a drawer is in a dresser. When the dresser is in the room. You may have the feeling that you are enlivening it.

8:07pm

House's shocking sameness. Floorboards 8:08pm wood table. Wall-to-wall. Surface throughout either inside or outside of 8:09pm the house.

Need be sentient thinks 8:10pm you don't know what the formula is. Seven or eight walks per week or sometimes not exiting the vessel. Things stay the same while tempting new behaviors.

Make a horizontal emotion. Motion log solidified and dispersed tension. Surfaces get bothered. There is 8:11pm a house to return to. Psychologically making a comfort. Here. Having arrived at the center. The difference between *moving through* and *retained for the records*.

"Excess emotion" should you keep it hidden or field it based on the charge of the release? A house not unlike a mutable equation. A tonic for whatever's enclosed the whole you melt without even warning stop. It felt similar to a walk only you mistook street level for an archive of emotions horizontally laid out.

They are horizontally laid out. You can choose. To fold and unfold during 8:12pm. The house is *a find*. The system collapses. Keep moving through. Weigh and retain for the records. Can choose to increase storage capacity at 8:13pm. Now you're in the compartment.

TINCTURED WITH LUNACY II

f
folk medicine (x, 7, 109,
See also Society) finds liquid
at home in alchemical impulse
see-through pieces wash up
dear masculine stone, remove block
ages relieve shakes Au of folk meds
of the periodic table later on Au of
Au matte warmth or a sheer curtain
in body-mind neediness table or the
periodic table itself like a nest

changing metal, froth a base into
gold a base into gold or something
one energized energize enter pull
from whatever's around

froth (3, 11, 36, 40, 41, 55, 58, 87,
89–91, 97, 101, 115, 144, 180, 196)
aligned with healer in the changing
from matte to gloss in frothy mug of

f
usages though minded yawn
the mind urged with what

nothing

in certain frequencies of meditation

frequent rigor of a headache, 26

as within.......here and there is a

vessel of gold and a sidewalk

E searches and sips this "elixir

of life" and on page seven of a book

reads about skin glowing from gold

yawning, yellow what heard? energized

tonic in the mind cloud the pendant in the

shape of the hue of a lamp handmade crush

crushing the dust into something bioavailable

f
of found glint properties of the plant

horizontally

the dry mind neurological cautions

dear use of a vessel enter that play

annexed and then dropped down

in pieces she in sheer confusing it with

the windows swung open in the vestibule

E,

E,

E,

in the compartment changing

a base metal into gold such a

forerunner levity crystalline a

claim to be a form or forming

vulgar silver and vulgar gold

(

tasted mercury we mineral talk

anti-intelectual goings > the sum of all those

silvers and golds undone the toxicity and made
made

made

edible even pg 74 thin climate opening

when all the layers silvers and golds

smooth analysis she waves going

archetypes falling visually into

the opening of physical archive

like of this predisposition in mine

mind, practice, great work offered

a blackening

a whitening

a yellowing

a reddening

it's changed

/////////////////

new age

abstract the summit

sensorimotor gamma and lined quilt

just crawl arch into certainly next-life

E-being passed through the corpus whether

in existence or not "act madly" (342) or

"mad part" (342) indirect expel it

from each muscle that day post-

falling in pieces she in sameness

arched and keyed in begun again

to eat the silk of eggs falling sensory

and annex being a hard thing into

a soft thing into ////////////////////////

a hard thing into a soft thing into

a matte thing into a glossy thing

into a thing all wrapped and hidden

into a thing expanding on the wall

into a thing in a pile on the floor

call it a floating vestibule

but is what excess enough too

around ideas a foundational under

current arched, Arched, arched, Arch.

it and seems like a question of having

quilted the fall a long egg, sat meditate

the document was on the equinox fall but

each movement pinned to some airy place for just it

potion a muscular attack and then sheer release

post-matte and low and suspended no less than an egg move

about the quilt folded on the floor a towel a moving blanket

a bare pillow nonetheless it's not a risk but it's still arching

brainy sew due to silvers and golds: chocolate wrapper, aluminum foil, expression of emotion things are plated

an ion of gold Au

Au

An auric

phase, solid

nuggets and rocks

tasted metal in my mouth

due to electricity, 211, 216

the doctrine is resting

auric of E's surrounding

experiment carried out

here be the universal elixir

E begin to pour kitchen in

in transparency and green velum

and slowing now and the vent

NUMBERS
NUMBER
NUMB
ER
errant and the equaling
beginning Q? a potion

bracketed

muscular still extremely tired not checking the document's

emotional quotient E pouring and transmute the cure for each

disease has what "chemistry"? E refuses the periodic table

the table in the kitchen is round and centered and gridded

the solvent solving rewritten and quite simply

it is pacifying to the nervous system it is a potion made

from it is aligned and guided in the vestibule making a

tonic in the vestibule the desert all around the city just

floating E text am that and that and that from lead to gold

lower frequency to higher or a cure for this irritant E (empty)

IN THE COMPARTMENT

You are in a house attempting domesticity warding off hysteria and irresistible impulses. For instance, you've never been more aware of the weight of the brain on the neck.

You respect logic but can only take it so far before emotion seeps in, the wind at the start of the event. You would like to number your feelings and place them in miniature folders. Fold them and find an adequate compartment. An archive for the changes of the waves of the brain. The filing cabinet could live at the edge of the Atlantic Ocean and move in and out with the tide.

No, it would stand firm amidst the changing tides. It would be waterproof and benefit from saltwater. The color would change from deep green to lighter green. What was once clustered and dispersed would get compiled.

You would return daily to the object by the ocean and you alone would have the ability to use the information. The feelings inside interacting with each other in the dark.

Of course, the contents of the compartment shift.

What time is it?

You weren't removed from your body but weren't exactly in there, either. All around the edges shook. The porch at the front of the house and just beyond that, the filing cabinet where you'll place this and just beyond that, the ocean. The original waves.

The house is still intact. Brainwaves weigh nothing.

A text message received: *What's up?*

You gutted the house. The house with the view of the compartment. You had a strong feeling about it. Ownership, the word *love*. A showy house, an edge taken.

You think you can see the deep green filing cabinet from the attic window.

The man said, "because what is consciousness but a wave of the hand?"

A wave.

Avoid storms of any sort. Do not walk outside when it's windy. Move to a place where the temperature is consistent but still look at photographs of the seasons. Travel infrequently and prepare weeks ahead of time if the need arises. Follow the centuries old rule of living a temperate life.

The archive is wild.

The compartment should hold real answers. The emotional archive is your only boat.

Now that you're in the ocean, looking at the compartment from the other side, you're confused.

According to the man, logic is or had been more reliable than intuition. According to you, logic had never been more reliable than intuition.

Your body moves back and forth between the house and the ocean. You place thoughts in the compartment as you pass.

Near the dreary February ocean, you are choosing to live austerely.

You're swimming.

Accruing emotional documents requires labor. The man said, "some women are logical and you are not one of them."

You've never felt so clued in, so able to access the wave brain. You can inhabit the archive whenever you want.

The tumultuous she. The brainwaves looking sharp on the tundra. Especially you who. Were sought after, arranging the archive, going to just store it away or find a method for display. A whale moves in the night ocean.

Deeper inside the house, fresh white three-hundred-thread-count sheets.

The horizon is an imaginary line. The archive is vertical. The horizon is unchanging. The tides are changing. As in temperament. The body becomes more muscular, then softer. Forms and unforms. Steps between wave and archive. Words drip into water.

The house and the horizon with the compartment and the ocean in between.

Short-term memory: some loss.

Vitals: same-ish.

Condition: steady.

Patient: ruled more by emotion than by reason.

Decision: respected but not recommended.

It's always nice to talk to you. I like when you come in. Please do get sleep. After you wake up, it will be gone. You have a three percent chance of dying from your condition in the next ten years. At the rate you're going.

At the rate you're going. The brain is trainable.

Make a list of things that are trainable.

NOTES

All entries in "The Falling Sickness" are from *The Falling Sickness: A History of Epilepsy from the Greeks to the Beginnings of Modern Neurology* by Owsei Temkin and all page numbers that appear throughout *Wave Archive* correlate to this book.

"Tinctured with Lunacy" and "Tinctured with Lunacy II" reference Herbert Butterfield's 1949 statement that alchemists are at risk of becoming "tinctured with the kind of lunacy they set out to describe."

ACKNOWLEDGEMENTS

This book was written in bursts during the years 2013-2019 while I was living in Brooklyn and at the New Jersey shore. Epilepsy has been my greatest school and teacher, and this book was written before and after many grand mal seizures.

In addition to epilepsy, I have been helped in the writing of this book by speaking with my numerous healers and neurologists, friends, teachers, students, and clients, and by alchemy, astrology, and *The Falling Sickness*.

"Edge Document" first appeared on the Inpatient Press website (2015).
"To Forget the Self Is Called Entering Heaven" first appeared in *Gramma Poetry* (2018). Thanks to the editors of these publications.
"Trem" first appeared in *Gravel Projects, Issue 1: Sound*, curated by Audra Wolowiec.

Thanks to my friends and teachers from Pratt's MFA in Sculpture program, where I studied from 2014-2016, wrote much of this book, took the photographs, and made the cubes. Thanks also to the Lower Manhattan Cultural Council, where I was in residence from 2016-2017 and where much of this book was written while I looked at the East River.

I have endless gratitude for Julie Joosten, who chose this book and worked with me tirelessly, offering countless brilliant and generous edits. This book would be very different if not for her. Thanks to everyone at Book*hug, especially Jay and Hazel Millar, for their generous support and guidance.

Thanks to everyone at Ugly Duckling Presse, where I was working for much of the writing of this book, and to Daniel Owen and Michael Newton for being early readers and supporters.

Thanks to Valerie Wasser, Lindsey Bontempo, Joshua Fishbein, my parents, and the kind stranger on the subway, for catching me. Thanks especially to Ruthann

Russo, who indexed my seizures and to Joe and John Russo for their support and laughter. Thanks to my grandparents, Helen and Ed Mamrak, and thank you, Michael Newton, for everything and more. Thanks to Hanna, for grounding me.

This book is dedicated to John and Rosalie Russo and Vera Russo Reynolds.

PHOTO: JOHN RUSSO

EMMALEA RUSSO is the author of *G* (Futurepoem). She was a writer in residence at the Lower Manhattan Cultural Council and the 18th Street Arts Center (LA), and a visiting artist at the Art Academy of Cincinnati and Parsons School of Design. Recent writing has appeared in *Artcritical, BOMB, The Brooklyn Rail, Cosmopolitan, Hyperallergic,* and the *Los Angeles Review of Books.* Russo is a practicing astrologer and divides her time between Avon-by-the-Sea, NJ, and New York City.

COLOPHON

Manufactured as the first edition of *Wave Archive* in the fall of 2019 by Book*hug Press.

Edited for the press by Julie Joosten.
Copy edited by Mark Truscott.
Type + design by Malcolm Sutton.

Book*hug Press